Be Firm in Your Faith

Apostolic journey to Madrid on the
occasion of the 26th World Youth Day

*All booklets are published thanks to the
generous support of the members of the
Catholic Truth Society*

CATHOLIC TRUTH SOCIETY
PUBLISHERS TO THE HOLY SEE

Contents

Our deepest identity is in Christ

"Planted and built up in Jesus Christ, firm in the faith" (cf. *Col* 2:7)

At the source of your deepest aspirations

In every period of history, including our own, many young people experience a deep desire for personal relationships marked by truth and solidarity. Many of them yearn to build authentic friendships, to know true love, to start a family that will remain united, to achieve personal fulfilment and real security, all of which are the guarantee of a serene and happy future. In thinking of my own youth, I realize that stability and security are not the questions that most occupy the minds of young people. True enough, it is important to have a job and thus to have firm ground beneath our feet, yet the years of our youth are also a time when we are seeking to get the most out of life.

When I think back on that time, I remember above all that we were not willing to settle for a conventional middle-class life. We wanted something great, something new. We wanted to discover life itself, in all its grandeur and beauty. Naturally, part of that was due to the times we

lived in. During the Nazi dictatorship and the war, we were, so to speak, "hemmed in" by the dominant power structure. So we wanted to break out into the open, to experience the whole range of human possibilities. I think that, to some extent, this urge to break out of the ordinary is present in every generation.

Part of being young is desiring something beyond everyday life and a secure job, a yearning for something really truly greater. Is this simply an empty dream that fades away as we become older? No! Men and women were created for something great, for infinity. Nothing else will ever be enough. Saint Augustine was right when he said "our hearts are restless till they find their rest in you". The desire for a more meaningful life is a sign that God created us and that we bear his "imprint". God is life, and that is why every creature reaches out towards life. Because human beings are made in the image of God, we do this in a unique and special way. We reach out for love, joy and peace.

So we can see how absurd it is to think that we can truly live by removing God from the picture! God is the source of life. To set God aside is to separate ourselves from that source and, inevitably, to deprive ourselves of fulfilment and joy: "without the Creator, the creature fades into nothingness" (Second Vatican Council, *Gaudium et Spes*, 36). In some parts of the world, particularly in the West, today's culture tends to exclude

God, and to consider faith a purely private issue with no relevance for the life of society. Even though the set of values underpinning society comes from the Gospel – values like the sense of the dignity of the person, of solidarity, of work and of the family –, we see a certain "eclipse of God" taking place, a kind of amnesia which, albeit not an outright rejection of Christianity, is nonetheless a denial of the treasure of our faith, a denial that could lead to the loss of our deepest identity.

I encourage you to strengthen your faith in God, the Father of our Lord Jesus Christ. You are the future of society and of the Church! As the Apostle Paul wrote to the Christians of Colossae, it is vital to have roots, a solid foundation! This is particularly true today. Many people have no stable points of reference on which to build their lives, and so they end up deeply insecure. There is a growing mentality of relativism, which holds that everything is equally valid, that truth and absolute points of reference do not exist. But this way of thinking does not lead to true freedom, but rather to instability, confusion and blind conformity to the fads of the moment. As young people, you are entitled to receive from previous generations solid points of reference to help you to make choices and on which to build your lives: like a young plant which needs solid support until it can sink deep roots and become a sturdy tree capable of bearing fruit.

Planted and built up in Jesus Christ

In order to highlight the importance of faith in the lives of believers, I would like to reflect with you on each of the three terms used by Saint Paul in the expression: *"Planted and built up in Jesus Christ, firm in the faith"* (cf. *Col* 2:7). We can distinguish three images: "planted" calls to mind a tree and the roots that feed it; "built up" refers to the construction of a house; "firm" indicates growth in physical or moral strength. These images are very eloquent. Before commenting on them, I would like to point out that grammatically all three terms in the original text are in the passive voice. This means that it is Christ himself who takes the initiative to plant, build up and confirm the faithful.

The first image is that of a tree which is firmly planted thanks to its roots, which keep it upright and give it nourishment. Without those roots, it would be blown away by the wind and would die. What are our roots? Naturally our parents, our families and the culture of our country are very important elements of our personal identity. But the Bible reveals a further element. The prophet Jeremiah wrote: "Blessed are those who trust in the Lord, whose trust is the Lord. They shall be like a tree planted by water, sending out its roots by the stream. It shall not fear when heat comes, and its leaves shall stay green; in the year of drought it is not anxious, and it does not cease to bear fruit" (*Jer* 17:7-8). For the prophet, to send out roots means to put one's trust in God. From him we draw our life. Without him, we cannot truly live. "God gave us eternal life, and this life is in his Son" (1 *Jn* 5:11). Jesus himself tells us that he is our life (cf. *Jn* 14:6).

Consequently, Christian faith is not only a matter of believing that certain things are true, but above all a personal relationship with Jesus Christ. It is an encounter with the Son of God that gives new energy to the whole of our existence. When we enter into a personal relationship with him, Christ reveals our true identity and, in friendship with him, our life grows towards complete fulfilment.

There is a moment, when we are young, when each of us wonders: what meaning does my life have? What purpose and direction should I give to it? This is a very important moment, and it can worry us, perhaps for some time. We start wondering about the kind of work we should take up, the kind of relationships we should establish, the friendships we should cultivate... Here, once more, I think of my own youth. I was somehow aware quite early on that the Lord wanted me to be a priest. Then later, after the war, when I was in the seminary and at university on the way towards that goal, I had to recapture that certainty. I had to ask myself: is this really the path I was meant to take? Is this really God's will for me? Will I be able to remain faithful to him and completely at his service? A decision like this demands a certain struggle. It cannot be otherwise. But then came the certainty: this is the right thing! Yes, the Lord wants me, and he will give me strength. If I listen to him and walk with him, I become truly myself. What counts is not the fulfilment of my desires, but of his will. In this way life becomes authentic.

Just as the roots of a tree keep it firmly planted in the soil, so the foundations of a house give it long-lasting stability. Through faith, we have been built up in Jesus Christ (cf *Col* 2:7), even as a house is built on its foundations. Sacred history provides many examples of saints who built their lives on the word of God. The first is Abraham, our father in faith, who obeyed God when he was asked to leave his ancestral home and to set out for an unknown land. "Abraham believed God, and it was reckoned to him as righteousness, and he was called the friend of God" (*Jas* 2:23). Being built up in Jesus Christ means responding positively to God's call, trusting in him and putting his word into practice. Jesus himself reprimanded his disciples: "Why do you call me 'Lord, Lord', and do not do what I tell you?" (*Lk* 6:46). He went on to use the image of building a house: "I will show you what someone is like who comes to me, listens to my words, and acts on them. That one is like a person building a house, who dug deeply and laid the foundation on rock; when the flood came, the river burst against that house but could not shake it because it had been well built" (*Lk* 6:47-48).

Dear friends, build your own house on rock, just like the person who "dug deeply". Try each day to follow Christ's word. Listen to him as a true friend with whom you can share your path in life. With him at your side, you will find courage and hope to face difficulties and problems, and even to overcome disappointments and setbacks. You are constantly being offered easier choices, but you yourselves know that these are ultimately deceptive and cannot bring you serenity and joy. Only the word of God can show us the authentic way, and only the faith we have received is the light which shines on our path. Gratefully accept this spiritual gift which you have received from your families; strive to respond responsibly to God's call, and to grow in your faith. Do not believe those who tell you that you don't need others to build up your life! Find support in the faith of those who are dear to you, in the faith of the Church, and thank the Lord that you have received it and have made it your own!

Firm in the faith

You are *"planted and built up in Jesus Christ, firm in the faith"* (cf. *Col* 2:7). The Letter from which these words are taken was written by Saint Paul in order to respond to a specific need of the Christians in the city of Colossae. That community was threatened by the influence of certain cultural trends that were turning the faithful away from the Gospel. Our own cultural context, dear young

people, is not unlike that of the ancient Colossians.
Indeed, there is a strong current of secularist thought that
aims to make God marginal in the lives of people and
society by proposing and attempting to create a
"paradise" without him. Yet experience tells us that a
world without God becomes a "hell": filled with
selfishness, broken families, hatred between individuals
and nations, and a great deficit of love, joy and hope. On
the other hand, wherever individuals and nations accept
God's presence, worship him in truth and listen to his
voice, then the civilization of love is being built, a
civilization in which the dignity of all is respected, and
communion increases, with all its benefits. Yet some
Christians allow themselves to be seduced by secularism
or attracted by religious currents that draw them away
from faith in Jesus Christ. There are others who, while
not yielding to these enticements, have simply allowed
their faith to grow cold, with inevitable negative effects
on their moral lives.

To those Christians influenced by ideas alien to the
Gospel the Apostle Paul spoke of the power of Christ's
death and resurrection. This mystery is the foundation of
our lives and the centre of Christian faith. All
philosophies that disregard it and consider it
"foolishness" (1 *Cor* 1:23) reveal their limitations with
respect to the great questions deep in the hearts of human
beings. As the Successor of the Apostle Peter, I too want

to confirm you in the faith (cf. *Lk* 22:32). We firmly believe that Jesus Christ offered himself on the Cross in order to give us his love. In his passion, he bore our sufferings, took upon himself our sins, obtained forgiveness for us and reconciled us with God the Father, opening for us the way to eternal life. Thus we were freed from the thing that most encumbers our lives: the slavery of sin. We can love everyone, even our enemies, and we can share this love with the poorest of our brothers and sisters and all those in difficulty.

The Cross often frightens us because it seems to be a denial of life. In fact, the opposite is true! It is God's "yes" to mankind, the supreme expression of his love and the source from which eternal life flows. Indeed, it is from Jesus' heart, pierced on the Cross, that this divine life streamed forth, ever accessible to those who raise their eyes towards the Crucified One. I can only urge you, then, to embrace the Cross of Jesus, the sign of God's love, as the source of new life. Apart from Jesus Christ risen from the dead, there can be no salvation! He alone can free the world from evil and bring about the growth of the Kingdom of justice, peace and love to which we all aspire.

Believing in Jesus Christ without having seen him

In the Gospel we find a description of the Apostle Thomas's experience of faith when he accepted the mystery of the Cross and resurrection of Christ. Thomas was one of the twelve Apostles. He followed Jesus and was an eyewitness of his healings and miracles. He listened to his words, and he experienced dismay at Jesus' death. That Easter evening when the Lord appeared to the disciples, Thomas was not present. When he was told that Jesus was alive and had shown himself, Thomas stated: "Unless I see the mark of the nails in his hands, and put my finger in the mark of the nails and my hand in his side, I will not believe" (*Jn* 20:25).

We too want to be able to see Jesus, to speak with him and to feel his presence even more powerfully. For many people today, it has become difficult to approach Jesus. There are so many images of Jesus in circulation which, while claiming to be scientific, detract from his greatness and the uniqueness of his person. That is why, after many years of study and reflection, I thought of sharing something of my own personal encounter with Jesus by writing a book. It was a way to help others see, hear and touch the Lord in whom God came to us in order to make himself known. Jesus himself, when he appeared again to his disciples a week later, said to Thomas: "Put your finger here and see my hands. Reach out your hand and put it in my side. Do not doubt but believe" (*Jn* 20:27). We too can have tangible contact with Jesus and put our hand, so to speak, upon the signs of his Passion, the signs of his love. It is in the sacraments that he draws particularly near to us and gives himself to us. Dear young people, learn to "see" and to "meet" Jesus in the Eucharist, where he is present and close to us, and even becomes food for our journey. In the sacrament of Penance the Lord reveals his mercy and always grants us his forgiveness. Recognize and serve Jesus in the poor, the sick, and in our brothers and sisters who are in difficulty and in need of help.

Enter into a personal dialogue with Jesus Christ and cultivate it in faith. Get to know him better by reading the Gospels and the Catechism of the Catholic Church. Converse with him in prayer, and place your trust in him. He will never betray that trust! "Faith is first of all a *personal adherence* of man to God. At the same time, and inseparably, it is *a free assent to the whole truth that God has revealed*" (*Catechism of the Catholic Church*, 150). Thus you will acquire a mature and solid faith, one which will not be based simply on religious sentiment or on a vague memory of the catechism you studied as a child. You will come to know God and to live authentically in union with him, like the Apostle Thomas who showed his firm faith in Jesus in the words: "My Lord and my God!".

Sustained by the faith of the Church, in order to be witnesses

Jesus said to Thomas: "Have you believed because you have seen me? Blessed are those who have not seen and yet have come to believe" (*Jn* 20:29). He was thinking of the path the Church was to follow, based on the faith of eyewitnesses: the Apostles. Thus we come to see that our personal faith in Christ, which comes into being through dialogue with him, is bound to the faith of the Church. We do not believe as isolated individuals, but rather, through Baptism, we are members of this great family; it is the faith professed by the Church which reinforces our personal faith. The *Creed* that we proclaim at Sunday Mass protects us from the danger of believing in a God other than the one revealed by Christ: "Each believer is thus a link in the great chain of believers. I cannot believe without being carried by the faith of others, and by my faith I help support others in the faith" (*Catechism of the Catholic Church*, 166). Let us always thank the Lord for the gift of the Church, for the Church helps us to advance securely in the faith that gives us true life (cf. *Jn* 20:31).

In the history of the Church, the saints and the martyrs have always drawn from the glorious Cross of Christ the strength to be faithful to God even to the point of offering their own lives. In faith they found the strength to overcome their weaknesses and to prevail over every adversity. Indeed, as the Apostle John says, "Who is it that conquers the world but the one who believes that Jesus is the Son of God?" (1 *Jn* 5:5). The victory born of faith is that of love.

There have been, and still are, many Christians who are living witnesses of the power of faith that is expressed in charity. They have been peacemakers, promoters of justice and workers for a more humane world, a world in accordance with God's plan. With competence and professionalism, they have been committed in different sectors of the life of society, contributing effectively to the welfare of all. The charity that comes from faith led them to offer concrete witness by their actions and words. Christ is not a treasure meant for us alone; he is the most precious treasure we have, one that is meant to be shared with others. In our age of globalization, be witnesses of Christian hope all over the world. How many people long to receive this hope! Standing before the tomb of his friend Lazarus, who had died four days earlier, as he was about to call the dead man back to life, Jesus said to Lazarus' sister Martha: "If you believe, you will see the glory of God" (cf. *Jn* 11:40). In the same way, if you believe, and if you are able to live out your faith and bear witness to it every day, you will become a means of helping other young people like yourselves to find the meaning and joy of life, which is born of an encounter with Christ!

The strength of faith

... I have come here to meet thousands of young people from all over the world, Catholics committed to Christ searching for the truth that will give real meaning to their existence. I come as the Successor of Peter, to confirm them all in the faith, with days of intense pastoral activity, proclaiming that Jesus Christ is the way, the truth and the life; to motivate the commitment to build up the Kingdom of God in the world among us; to exhort young people to know Christ personally as a friend and so, rooted in his person, to become faithful followers and valiant witnesses.

Why has this multitude of young people come to Madrid? While they themselves should give the reply, it may be supposed that they wish to hear the word of God, as the motto for this World Youth Day proposed to them, in such a way that, rooted and built upon Christ, they may manifest the strength of their faith.

Many of them have heard the voice of God, perhaps only as a little whisper, which has led them to search for him more diligently and to share with others the experience of the force which he has in their lives. The discovery of the living God inspires young people and opens their eyes to the challenges of the world in which they live, with its possibilities and limitations. They see the prevailing superficiality, consumerism and hedonism, the widespread banalization of sexuality, the lack of solidarity, and the corruption. They know that, without God, it would be hard to confront these challenges and to be truly happy, and thus pouring out their enthusiasm in the attainment of an authentic life. But, with God beside them, they will possess light to walk by and reasons to hope, unrestrained before their highest ideals, which will motivate their generous commitment to build a society where human dignity and true brotherhood are respected.

A message of hope

Here on this Day, they have a special opportunity to gather together their aspirations, to share the richness of their cultures and experiences, motivate each other along a journey of faith and life, in which some think they are alone or ignored in their daily existence. But they are not alone. Many people of the same age have the same aspirations and, entrusting themselves completely to Christ, know that they really have a future before them and are not afraid of the decisive commitments which fulfil their entire lives. That is why it gives me great joy to listen to them, pray with them and celebrate the Eucharist with them. World Youth Day brings us a message of hope like a pure and youthful breeze, with rejuvenating scents which fill us with confidence before the future of the Church and the world.

Let nothing take away your peace

Of course, there is no lack of difficulties. There are tensions and ongoing conflicts all over the world, even to the shedding of blood. Justice and the unique value of the human person are easily surrendered to selfish, material and ideological interests. Nature and the environment, created by God with so much love, are not respected. Moreover, many young people look worriedly to the future, as they search for work, or because they have lost their job or because the one they have is precarious or uncertain. There are others who need help either to avoid drugs or to recover from their use. There are even some who, because of their faith in Christ, suffer discrimination which leads to contempt and persecution, open or hidden, which they endure in various regions and countries. They are harassed to give him up, depriving them of the signs of his presence in public life, not allowing even the mention of his holy name. But, with all my heart, I say again to you young people: let nothing and no one take away your peace; do not be ashamed of the Lord. He did not spare himself in becoming one like us and in experiencing our anguish so as to lift it up to God, and in this way he saved us.

In this regard, the young followers of Jesus must be aided to remain firm in the faith and to embrace the beautiful adventure of proclaiming it and witnessing to it openly with their lives. A witness that is courageous and full of love for their brothers and sisters, resolute and at the same time prudent, without hiding its Christian identity, living together with other legitimate choices in a spirit of respect while at the same time demanding due respect for one's own choices.

Our foundations are in Christ

There are words which serve only to amuse, as fleeting as an empty breeze; others, to an extent, inform us; those of Jesus, on the other hand, must reach our hearts, take root and bloom there all our lives. If not, they remain empty and become ephemeral. They do not bring us to him and, as a result, Christ stays remote, just one voice among the many others around us which are so familiar. Furthermore, the Master who speaks teaches, not something learned from others, but that which he himself is, the only one who truly knows the path of man towards God, because he is the one who opened it up for us, he made it so that we might have authentic lives, lives which are always worth living, in every circumstance, and which not even death can destroy. The Gospel continues, explaining these things with the evocative image of someone who builds on solid rock, resistant to the onslaught of adversity, and in contrast to someone who builds on sand - we would say today in what appears a paradise - but which collapses with the first gust of wind and falls into ruins.

Nourish your being

Listen closely to the words of the Lord, that they may be for you "spirit and life" (*Jn* 6:63), roots which nourish your being, a rule of life which likens us - poor in spirit, thirsting for justice, merciful, pure in heart, lovers of peace - to the person of Christ. Listen regularly every day as if he were the one friend who does not deceive, the one with whom we wish to share the path of life. Of course, you know that when we do not walk beside Christ our guide, we get lost on other paths, like the path of our blind and selfish impulses, or the path of flattering but self-serving suggestions, deceiving and fickle, which leave emptiness and frustration in their wake.

Rooted in Christ

Use these days to know Christ better and to make sure that, rooted in him, your enthusiasm and happiness, your desire to go further, to reach the heights, even God himself, always hold a sure future, because the fullness of life has already been placed within you. Let that life grow with divine grace, generously and without half-measures, as you remain steadfast in your aim for holiness. And, in the face of our weaknesses which sometimes overwhelm us, we can rely on the mercy of the Lord who is always ready to help us again and who offers us pardon in the sacrament of Penance.

Build on solid rock

If you build on solid rock, not only your life will be solid and stable, but it will also help project the light of Christ shining upon those of your own age and upon the whole of humanity, presenting a valid alternative to all those who have fallen short, because the essentials in their lives were inconsistent; to all those who are content to follow fashionable ideas, they take shelter in the here and now, forgetting true justice, or they take refuge in their own opinions instead of seeking the simple truth.

Indeed, there are many who, creating their own gods, believe they need no roots or foundations other than themselves. They take it upon themselves to decide what is true or not, what is good and evil, what is just and unjust; who should live and who can be sacrificed in the interests of other preferences; leaving each step to chance, with no clear path, letting themselves be led by the whim of each moment. These temptations are always lying in wait. It is important not to give in to them because, in reality, they lead to something so evanescent, like an existence with no horizons, a liberty without God. We, on the other hand, know well that we have been created free, in the image of God, precisely so that we might be in the forefront of the search for truth and goodness, responsible for our actions, not mere blind executives, but creative co-workers in the task of cultivating and beautifying the work of creation. God is looking for a responsible interlocutor, someone who can dialogue with him and love him. Through Christ we can truly succeed and, established in him, we give wings to our freedom. Is this not the great reason for our joy? Isn't this the firm ground upon which to build the civilization of love and life, capable of humanizing all of us?

Your happiness will influence others

Be prudent and wise; build your lives upon the firm foundation which is Christ. This wisdom and prudence will guide your steps, nothing will make you fear and peace will reign in your hearts. Then you will be blessed and happy and your happiness will influence others. They will wonder what the secret of your life is and they will discover that the rock which underpins the entire building and upon which rests your whole existence is the very person of Christ, your friend, brother and Lord, the Son of God incarnate, who gives meaning to the entire universe.

He died for us all, rising that we might have life, and now, from the throne of the Father, he accompanies all men and women, watching continually over each one of us.

Consecrated to Christ with an undivided heart

Dear Young Women Religious, as part of the World Youth Day which we are celebrating in Madrid, I am delighted to have this opportunity to meet you who have consecrated your youth to the Lord, and I thank you for the kind greeting you have given me. I also thank the Archbishop of Madrid, who arranged for this meeting in the evocative setting of the Monastery of San Lorenzo de El Escorial. Its famous library preserves important editions of the sacred Scriptures and the monastic rules of various religious families, yet your own lives of fidelity to the calling you have received is itself a precious means of preserving the word of the Lord, which resounds in your various spiritual traditions.

Every charism is an evangelical word which the Holy Spirit recalls to the Church's memory (cf. *Jn* 14:26). It is not by accident that consecrated life "is born from hearing the word of God and embracing the Gospel as its rule of life. A life devoted to following Christ in his chastity, poverty and obedience becomes a living 'exegesis' of God's word... Every charism and every rule springs from it and seeks to be an expression of it, thus opening up new pathways of Christian living marked by the radicalism of the Gospel" (*Verbum Domini*, 83).

An undivided heart

This Gospel radicalism means being "rooted and built up in Christ and firm in the faith" (cf. *Col* 2:7). In the consecrated life, this means going to the very root of the love of Jesus Christ with an undivided heart, putting nothing ahead of this love (cf. Saint Benedict, *Rule*, IV, 21) and being completely devoted to him, the Bridegroom, as were the Saints, like Rose of Lima and Rafael Arnáiz, the young patrons of this World Youth Day. Your lives must testify to the personal encounter with Christ which has nourished your consecration, and to all the transforming power of that encounter. This is all the more important today when "we see a certain 'eclipse of God' taking place, a kind of amnesia which, albeit not an outright rejection of Christianity, is nonetheless a denial of the treasure of our faith, a denial that could lead to the loss of our deepest identity" (*Message for the 2011 World Youth Day*, 1). In a world of relativism and mediocrity, we need that radicalism to which your consecration, as a way of belonging to the God who is loved above all things, bears witness.

This Gospel radicalism proper to the consecrated life finds expression in filial communion with the Church, the home of the children of God, built by Christ:

communion with her Pastors who set forth in the Lord's name the deposit of faith received from the apostles, the ecclesial Magisterium and the Christian tradition; communion with your own religious families as you gratefully preserve their authentic spiritual patrimony while valuing other charisms; and communion with other members of the Church, such as the laity, who are called to make their own specific calling a testimony to the one Gospel of the Lord.

The seed of the Gospel bears fruit

Finally, Gospel radicalism finds expression in the mission God has chosen to entrust to us: from the contemplative life, which welcomes into its cloisters the word of God in eloquent silence and adores his beauty in the solitude which he alone fills, to the different paths of the apostolic life, in whose furrows the seed of the Gospel bears fruit in the education of children and young people, the care of the sick and elderly, the pastoral care of families, commitment to respect for life, witness to the truth and the proclamation of peace and charity, mission work and the new evangelization, and so many other sectors of the Church's apostolate.

This is the witness of holiness to which God is calling you, as you follow Jesus Christ closely and unconditionally in consecration, communion and mission. The Church needs your youthful fidelity, rooted and built

up in Christ. Thank you for your generous, total and perpetual "yes" to the call of the Loved One. I pray that the Virgin Mary may sustain and accompany your consecrated youth, with the lively desire that it will challenge, nourish and illumine all young people.

With these sentiments, I ask God to repay abundantly the generous contribution which consecrated life has made to this World Youth Day. In his name, and with great gratitude, I give you my affectionate blessing.

Spreading the truth of Christ

I have looked forward to this meeting with you, young professors in the universities of Spain. You provide a splendid service in the spread of truth, in circumstances that are not always easy...

I am reminded of my own first steps as a professor at the University of Bonn. At the time, the wounds of war were still deeply felt and we had many material needs; these were compensated by our passion for an exciting activity, our interaction with colleagues of different disciplines and our desire to respond to the deepest and most basic concerns of our students. This experience of a "Universitas" of professors and students who together seek the truth in all fields of knowledge, or as Alfonso X the Wise put it, this "counsel of masters and students with the will and understanding needed to master the various disciplines" (*Siete Partidas*, partida II, tit. XXXI), helps us to see more clearly the importance, and even the definition, of the University.

The theme of the present World Youth Day – "Rooted and Built Up in Christ, and Firm in the Faith" (cf. *Col* 2:7) can also shed light on your efforts to understand more clearly your own identity and what you are called to do. As I wrote in my Message to Young People in preparation for these days, the terms "rooted, built up and firm" all point to solid foundations on which we can construct our lives (cf. No. 2).

The authentic idea of the University

But where will young people encounter those reference points in a society which is increasingly confused and unstable? At times one has the idea that the mission of a university professor nowadays is exclusively that of forming competent and efficient professionals capable of satisfying the demand for labour at any given time. One also hears it said that the only thing that matters at the present moment is pure technical ability. This sort of utilitarian approach to education is in fact becoming more widespread, even at the university level, promoted especially by sectors outside the University. All the same, you who, like myself, have had an experience of the University, and now are members of the teaching staff, surely are looking for something more lofty and capable of embracing the full measure of what it is to be human. We know that when mere utility and pure pragmatism become the principal criteria, much is lost and the results can be tragic: from the abuses associated with a science which acknowledges no limits beyond itself, to the political totalitarianism which easily arises when one eliminates any higher reference than the mere calculus of power. The authentic idea of the University, on the other hand, is precisely what saves us from this reductionist and curtailed vision of humanity.

In truth, the University has always been, and is always called to be, the "house" where one seeks the truth proper to the human person. Consequently it was not by accident that the Church promoted the universities, for Christian faith speaks to us of Christ as the Word through whom all things were made (cf. *Jn* 1:3) and of men and women as made in the image and likeness of God. The Gospel message perceives a rationality inherent in creation and considers man as a creature participating in, and capable of attaining to, an understanding of this rationality. The University thus embodies an ideal which must not be attenuated or compromised, whether by ideologies closed to reasoned dialogue or by truckling to a purely utilitarian and economic conception which would view man solely as a consumer.

Seeking and encountering truth

Here we see the vital importance of your own mission. You yourselves have the honour and responsibility of transmitting the ideal of the University: an ideal which you have received from your predecessors, many of whom were humble followers of the Gospel and, as such, became spiritual giants. We should feel ourselves their successors, in a time quite different from their own, yet one in which the essential human questions continue to challenge and stimulate us. With them, we realize that we are a link in that chain of men and women committed to teaching the faith and making it credible to human reason. And we do this not simply by our teaching, but by the way we live our faith and embody it, just as the Word took flesh and dwelt among us. Young people need authentic teachers: persons open to the fullness of truth in the various branches of knowledge, persons who listen to and experience in own hearts that interdisciplinary dialogue; persons who, above all, are convinced of our human capacity to advance along the path of truth. Youth is a privileged time for seeking and encountering truth. As Plato said: "Seek truth while you are young, for if you do not, it will later escape your grasp" (*Parmenides*, 135d). This lofty aspiration is the most precious gift which you can give to your students, personally and by example. It is more important than mere technical know-how, or cold and purely functional data.

I urge you, then, never to lose that sense of enthusiasm and concern for truth. Always remember that teaching is not just about communicating content, but about forming young people. You need to understand and love them, to awaken their innate thirst for truth and their yearning for transcendence. Be for them a source of encouragement and strength.

For this to happen, we need to realize in the first place that the path to the fullness of truth calls for complete commitment: it is a path of understanding and love, of reason and faith. We cannot come to know something unless we are moved by love; or, for that matter, love something which does not strike us as reasonable. "Understanding and love are not in separate compartments: love is rich in understanding and understanding is full of love" (*Caritas in Veritate*, 30). If truth and goodness go together, so too do knowledge and love. This unity leads to consistency in life and thought, that ability to inspire demanded of every good educator.

In the second place, we need to recognize that truth itself will always lie beyond our grasp. We can seek it and draw near to it, but we cannot completely possess it; or put better, truth possesses us and inspires us. In intellectual and educational activity the virtue of humility is also indispensable, since it protects us from the pride which bars the way to truth. We must not draw students to ourselves, but set them on the path toward the truth which we seek together. The Lord will help you in this, for he asks you to be plain and effective like salt, or like the lamp which quietly lights the room (cf. *Mt* 5:13).

Seat of wisdom

All these things, finally, remind us to keep our gaze fixed on Christ, whose face radiates the Truth which enlightens us. Christ is also the Way which leads to lasting fulfilment; he walks constantly at our side and sustains us with his love. Rooted in him, you will prove good guides to our young people. With this confidence I invoke upon you the protection of the Virgin Mary, Seat of Wisdom. May she help you to cooperate with her Son by living a life which is personally satisfying and which brings forth rich fruits of knowledge and faith for your students. Thank you very much.

Mysterious wisdom of the Cross

We have celebrated this Way of the Cross with fervour and devotion, following Christ along the path of his passion and death. The commentaries of the Little Sisters of the Cross, who serve the poor and most needy, have helped us enter into the mystery of Christ's glorious Cross, wherein is found God's true wisdom which judges the world and judges those who consider themselves wise (cf. *1 Cor* 1:17-19). We have also been assisted on this journey to Calvary by our contemplation of these wonderful images from the religious patrimony of the Spanish dioceses. In these images, faith and art combine so as to penetrate our heart and summon us to conversion. When faith's gaze is pure and authentic, beauty places itself at its service and is able to depict the mysteries of our salvation in such a way as to move us profoundly and transform our hearts, as Saint Teresa of Jesus herself experienced while contemplating an image of the wounded Christ (cf. *Autobiography*, 9:1).

As we were making our way with Jesus towards the place of his sacrifice on Mount Calvary, the words of Saint Paul came to mind: "Christ loved me and gave himself for me" (*Gal* 2:20). In the face of such disinterested love, we find ourselves asking, filled with wonder and gratitude: What can we do for him? What response shall we give him? Saint John puts it succinctly: "By this we know love, that he laid down his life for us; and we ought to lay down our lives for the brethren" (*1 Jn* 3:16). Christ's passion urges us to take upon our own shoulders the sufferings of the world, in the certainty that God is not distant or far removed from man and his troubles. On the contrary, he became one of us "in order to *suffer with* man in an utterly real way — in flesh and blood ... hence in all human suffering we are joined by one who experiences and carries that suffering *with* us; hence *con-solatio* is present in all suffering, the consolation of God's compassionate love — and so the star of hope rises" (*Spe Salvi*, 39).

May Christ's love for us increase your joy and encourage you to go in search of those less fortunate. You are open to the idea of sharing your lives with others, so be sure not to pass by on the other side in the face of human suffering, for it is here that God expects you to give of your very best: your capacity for love and compassion. The different forms of suffering that have unfolded before our eyes in the course of this Way of the Cross are the Lord's way of summoning us to spend our lives following in his footsteps and becoming signs of his consolation and salvation. "To suffer with the other and for others; to suffer for the sake of truth and justice; to suffer out of love and in order to become a person who truly loves — these are fundamental elements of humanity, and to abandon them would destroy man himself" (*ibid.*).

Let us eagerly welcome these teachings and put them into practice. Let us look upon Christ, hanging on the harsh wood of the Cross, and let us ask him to teach us this mysterious wisdom of the Cross, by which man lives. The Cross was not a sign of failure, but an expression of self-giving in love that extends even to the supreme sacrifice of one's life. The Father wanted to show his love for us through the embrace of his crucified Son: crucified out of love. The Cross, by its shape and its meaning, represents this love of both the Father and the Son for men. Here we recognize the icon of supreme love, which teaches us to love what God loves and in the way that he loves: this is the Good News that gives hope to the world.

Let us turn our gaze now to the Virgin Mary, who was given to us on Calvary to be our Mother, and let us ask her to sustain us with her loving protection along the path of life, particularly when we pass through the night of suffering, so that we may be able to remain steadfast, as she did, at the foot of the Cross.

Prepare to become Apostles

I am very pleased to celebrate Holy Mass with you who aspire to be Christ's priests for the service of the Church and of man, and I thank you for the kind words with which you welcomed me. Today, this holy cathedral church of Santa María La Real de la Almudena is like a great Upper Room, where the Lord greatly desires to celebrate the Passover with you who wish one day to preside in his name at the mysteries of salvation. Looking at you, I again see proof of how Christ continues to call young disciples and to make them his apostles, thus keeping alive the mission of the Church and the offer of the Gospel to the world. As seminarians you are on the path towards a sacred goal: to continue the mission which Christ received from the Father. Called by him, you have followed his voice and, attracted by his loving gaze, you now advance towards the sacred ministry. Fix your eyes upon him who through his incarnation is the supreme revelation of God to the world and who through his resurrection faithfully fulfils his promise. Give thanks to him for this sign of favour in which he holds each one of you.

The first reading which we heard shows us Christ as the new and eternal priest who made of himself a perfect offering. The response to the psalm may be aptly applied to him since, at his coming into the world, he said to the Father, "Here I am to do your will" (cf. *Ps* 39:8). He tried to please him in all things: in his words and actions, along the way or welcoming sinners. His life was one of service and his longing was a constant prayer, placing himself in the name of all before the Father as the first-born son of many brothers and sisters. The author of the Letter to the Hebrews states that, by a single offering, he brought to perfection for all time those of us who are called to share his sonship (cf. *Heb* 10:14).

The Eucharist, whose institution is mentioned in the Gospel just proclaimed (cf. *Lk* 22:14-20), is the real expression of that unconditional offering of Jesus for all, even for those who betrayed him. It was the offering of his body and blood for the life of mankind and for the forgiveness of sins. His blood, a sign of life, was given to us by God as a covenant, so that we might apply the force of his life wherever death reigns due to our sins, and thus destroy it. Christ's body broken and his blood outpoured – the surrender of his freedom – became through these Eucharistic signs the new source of mankind's redeemed freedom. In Christ, we have the promise of definitive redemption and the certain hope of future blessings. Through Christ we know that we are not walking towards the abyss, the silence of nothingness or death, but are rather pilgrims on the way to a promised land, on the way to him who is our end and our beginning.

You are preparing yourselves to become apostles with Christ and like Christ, and to accompany your fellow men and women along their journey as companions and servants.

How should you behave during these years of preparation? First of all, they should be years of interior silence, of unceasing prayer, of constant study and of gradual insertion into the pastoral activity and structures of the Church. A Church which is community and institution, family and mission, the creation of Christ through his Holy Spirit, as well as the result of those of us who shape it through our holiness and our sins. God, who does not hesitate to make of the poor and of sinners his friends and instruments for the redemption of the human race, willed it so. The holiness of the Church is above all the objective holiness of the very person of Christ, of his Gospel and his sacraments, the holiness of that power from on high which enlivens and impels it. We have to be saints so as not to create a contradiction between the sign that we are and the reality that we wish to signify.

Love and realism

Meditate well upon this mystery of the Church, living the years of your formation in deep joy, humbly, clear-mindedly and with radical fidelity to the Gospel, in an affectionate relation to the time spent and the people among whom you live. No one chooses the place or the people to whom he is sent, and every time has its own challenges; but in every age God gives the right grace to face and overcome those challenges with love and realism. That is why, no matter the circumstances in which he finds and however difficult they may be, the priest must grow in all kinds of good works, keeping alive within him the words spoken on his Ordination day, by which he was exhorted to model his life on the mystery of the Lord's cross.

Modelled on Christ

To be modelled on Christ, dear seminarians, is to be identified ever more closely with him who, for our sake, became servant, priest and victim. To be modelled on him is in fact the task upon which the priest spends his entire life. We already know that it is beyond us and we will not fully succeed but, as St Paul says, we run towards the goal, hoping to reach it (cf. *Phil* 3:12-14).

That said, Christ the High Priest is also the Good Shepherd who cares for his sheep, even giving his life for them (cf. *Jn* 10:11). In order to liken yourselves to the Lord in this as well, your heart must mature while in seminary, remaining completely open to the Master. This openness, which is a gift of the Holy Spirit, inspires the decision to live in celibacy for the sake of the kingdom of heaven and, leaving aside the world's goods, live in austerity of life and sincere obedience, without pretence.

Gratuitousness and service

Ask him to let you imitate him in his perfect charity towards all, so that you do not shun the excluded and sinners, but help them convert and return to the right path. Ask him to teach you how to be close to the sick and the poor in simplicity and generosity. Face this challenge without anxiety or mediocrity, but rather as a beautiful way of living our human life in gratuitousness and service, as witnesses of God made man, messengers of the supreme dignity of the human person and therefore its unconditional defenders. Relying on his love, do not be intimidated by surroundings that would exclude God and in which power, wealth and pleasure are frequently the main criteria ruling people's lives. You may be shunned along with others who propose higher goals or who unmask the false gods before whom many now bow down. That will be the moment when a life deeply rooted in Christ will clearly be seen as something new and it will powerfully attract those who truly search for God, truth and justice.

A path demanding courage and authenticity

Under the guidance of your formators, open your hearts to the light of the Lord, to see if this path which demands

courage and authenticity is for you. Approach the priesthood only if you are firmly convinced that God is calling you to be his ministers, and if you are completely determined to exercise it in obedience to the Church's precepts.

With this confidence, learn from him who described himself as meek and humble of heart, leaving behind all earthly desire for his sake so that, rather than pursuing your own good, you build up your brothers and sisters by the way you live, as did the patron saint of the diocesan clergy of Spain, St John of Avila. Moved by his example, look above all to the Virgin Mary, Mother of Priests. She will know how to mould your hearts according to the model of Christ, her divine Son, and she will teach you how to treasure for ever all that he gained on Calvary for the salvation of the world.

How to embrace suffering

I thank you most sincerely for your kind greeting and heartfelt welcome. This evening, just before the Prayer Vigil with the young people from throughout the world gathered in Madrid for this World Youth Day, we have this chance to spend time together as a way of showing the Pope's closeness and esteem for each of you, for your families and for all those who help and care for you in this Foundation of Saint Joseph's Institute.

Youth, as I have said more than once, is the age when life discloses itself to us with all its rich possibilities, inspiring us to seek the lofty goals which give it meaning. So when suffering appears on the horizon of a young life, we are shaken; perhaps we ask ourselves: "Can life still be something grand, even when suffering unexpectedly enters it?" In my Encyclical on Christian Hope, I observed that "the true measure of humanity is essentially determined in relationship to suffering and to the sufferer ... A society unable to accept its suffering members and incapable of helping to share their suffering and to bear it inwardly through 'compassion' is a cruel and inhuman society" (*Spe Salvi*, 38). These words reflect a long tradition of humanity which arises from Christ's own self-offering on the Cross for us and for our redemption. Jesus and, in his footsteps, his Sorrowful Mother and the saints, are witnesses who shows us how to experience the tragedy of suffering for our own good and for the salvation of the world.

The look of love

These witnesses speak to us, first and foremost, of the dignity of all human life, created in the image of God. No suffering can efface this divine image imprinted in the depths of our humanity. But there is more: because the Son of God wanted freely to embrace suffering and death, we are also capable of seeing God's image in the face of those who suffer. This preferential love of the Lord for the suffering helps us to see others more clearly and to give them, above and beyond their material demands, the look of love which they need. But this can only happen as the fruit of a personal encounter with Christ. You yourselves – as religious, family members, health care professionals and volunteers who daily live and work with these young people – know this well. Your lives and your committed service proclaim the greatness to which every human being is called: to show compassion and loving concern to the suffering, just as God himself did. In your noble work we hear an echo of the words found in the Gospel: "just as you did it to one of the least of these my brothers, you did it to me" (*Mt* 25:40).

A tenderness which opens us to salvation

At the same time, you are also witnesses of the immense goodness which the lives of these young people represent for those who love them, and for humanity as a whole. In a mysterious yet real way, their presence awakens in our often hardened hearts a tenderness which opens us to salvation. The lives of these young people surely touch human hearts and for that reason we are grateful to the Lord for having known them.

The civilization of love

Our society, which all too often questions the inestimable value of life, of every life, needs you: in a decisive way you help to build the civilization of love. What is more, you play a leading role in that civilization. As sons and daughters of the Church, you offer the Lord your lives, with all their ups and downs, cooperating with him and somehow becoming "part of the treasury of compassion so greatly needed by the human race" (*Spe Salvi*, 40).

With great affection, and through the intercession of Saint Joseph, Saint John of God and Saint Benito Menni, I commend you to God our Lord: may he be your strength and your reward. As a pledge of his love, I cordially impart to you, and to your families and friends, my Apostolic Blessing.

Faith elevates and perfects your ideals

Your concerns express the longing which all of you have to achieve something great in life, something which can bring you fulfilment and happiness.

How can a young person be true to the faith and yet continue to aspire to high ideals in today's society? In the Gospel we have just heard, Jesus gives us an answer to this urgent question: "As the Father has loved me, so I have loved you; abide in my love" (*Jn* 15:9).

Yes, dear friends, God loves us. This is the great truth of our life; it is what makes everything else meaningful. We are not the product of blind chance or absurdity; instead our life originates as part of a loving plan of God. To abide in his love, then, means living a life rooted in faith, since faith is more than the mere acceptance of certain abstract truths: it is an intimate relationship with Christ, who enables us to open our hearts to this mystery of love and to live as men and women conscious of being loved by God.

The source of true happiness and joy

If you abide in the love of Christ, rooted in the faith, you will encounter, even amid setbacks and suffering, the source of true happiness and joy. Faith does not run counter to your highest ideals; on the contrary, it elevates and perfects those ideals. Dear young people, do not be satisfied with anything less than Truth and Love, do not be content with anything less than Christ.

Let no adversity paralyze you

Nowadays, although the dominant culture of relativism all around us has given up on the search for truth, even if it is the highest aspiration of the human spirit, we need to speak with courage and humility of the universal significance of Christ as the Saviour of humanity and the source of hope for our lives. He who took upon himself our afflictions, is well acquainted with the mystery of human suffering and manifests his loving presence in those who suffer. They in their turn, united to the passion of Christ, share closely in his work of redemption. Furthermore, our disinterested attention towards the sick and the forgotten will always be a humble and warm testimony of God's compassionate regard.

Dear friends, may no adversity paralyze you. Be afraid neither of the world, nor of the future, nor of your weakness. The Lord has allowed you to live in this moment of history so that, by your faith, his name will continue to resound throughout the world.

Find your vocation in society

During this prayer vigil, I urge you to ask God to help you find your vocation in society and in the Church, and to persevere in that vocation with joy and fidelity. It is a good thing to open our hearts to Christ's call and to follow with courage and generosity the path he maps out for us.

The Lord calls many people to marriage, in which a man and a woman, in becoming one flesh (cf. *Gen* 2:24), find fulfilment in a profound life of communion. It is a prospect that is both bright and demanding. It is a project for true love which is daily renewed and deepened by sharing joys and sorrows, one marked by complete self-giving. For this reason, to acknowledge the beauty and goodness of marriage is to realize that only a setting of fidelity and indissolubility, along with openness to God's gift of life, is adequate to the grandeur and dignity of marital love.

Christ calls others to follow him more closely in the priesthood or in consecrated life. It is hard to put into words the happiness you feel when you know that Jesus seeks you, trusts in you, and with his unmistakable voice also says to you: "Follow me!" (cf. *Mk* 2:14).

Remain in his love as his friends

If you wish to discover and to live faithfully the form of life to which the Lord is calling each of you, you must remain in his love as his friends. And how do we preserve friendship except through frequent contact, conversation, being together in good times and bad? Saint Teresa of Jesus used to say that prayer is just such "friendly contact, often spending time alone with the one who we know loves us" (cf. *Autobiography*, 8).

And so I now ask you to "abide" in the adoration of Christ, truly present in the Eucharist. I ask you to enter into conversation with him, to bring before him your questions and to listen to his voice. I pray for you with all my heart. And I ask you to pray for me. Let us ask the Lord to grant that, attracted by the beauty of his love, we may always live faithfully as his disciples.

I thank you for your joy and your resistance. Your strength is greater than the rain. Thank you. With rain the Lord has sent us many blessings. In this also, you are an example.

Ways of knowing Christ

In this celebration of the Eucharist we have reached the high point of this World Youth Day. Seeing you here, gathered in such great numbers from all parts of the world, fills my heart with joy. I think of the special love with which Jesus is looking upon you. Yes, the Lord loves you and calls you his friends (cf. *Jn* 15:15). He goes out to meet you and he wants to accompany you on your journey, to open the door to a life of fulfilment and to give you a share in his own closeness to the Father. For our part, we have come to know the immensity of his love and we want to respond generously to his love by sharing with others the joy we have received. Certainly, there are many people today who feel attracted by the figure of Christ and want to know him better. They realize that he is the answer to so many of our deepest concerns. But who is he really? How can someone who lived on this earth so long ago have anything in common with me today?

Impersonal knowledge

The Gospel we have just heard (cf. *Mt* 16:13-20) suggests two different ways of knowing Christ. The first is an impersonal knowledge, one based on current opinion.

When Jesus asks: "Who do people say that the Son of Man is?", the disciples answer: "Some say John the Baptist, but others Elijah, and still others Jeremiah or one of the prophets". In other words, Christ is seen as yet another religious figure, like those who came before him. Then Jesus turns to the disciples and asks them: "But who do you say that I am?" Peter responds with what is the first confession of faith: "You are the Messiah, the Son of the living God". Faith is more than just empirical or historical facts; it is an ability to grasp the mystery of Christ's person in all its depth.

A gift of God

Yet faith is not the result of human effort, of human reasoning, but rather a gift of God: "Blessed are you, Simon son of Jonah! For flesh and blood has not revealed this to you, but my Father in heaven". Faith starts with God, who opens his heart to us and invites us to share in his own divine life. Faith does not simply provide information about who Christ is; rather, it entails a personal relationship with Christ, a surrender of our whole person, with all our understanding, will and feelings, to God's self-revelation. So Jesus' question: "But who do you say that I am?", is ultimately a challenge to the disciples to make a personal decision in his regard. Faith in Christ and discipleship are strictly interconnected.

And, since faith involves following the Master, it must become constantly stronger, deeper and more mature, to the extent that it leads to a closer and more intense relationship with Jesus. Peter and the other disciples also had to grow in this way, until their encounter with the Risen Lord opened their eyes to the fullness of faith.

"Who do you say that I am?"

Today Christ is asking you the same question which he asked the Apostles: "Who do you say that I am?" Respond to him with generosity and courage, as befits young hearts like your own. Say to him: "Jesus, I know that you are the Son of God, who have given your life for me. I want to follow you faithfully and to be led by your word. You know me and you love me. I place my trust in you and I put my whole life into your hands. I want you to be the power that strengthens me and the joy which never leaves me".

The rock of faith

Jesus' responds to Peter's confession by speaking of the Church: "And I tell you, you are Peter, and on this rock I will build my Church". What do these words mean? Jesus builds the Church on the rock of the faith of Peter, who confesses that Christ is God.

The Church, then, is not simply a human institution, like any other. Rather, she is closely joined to God. Christ himself speaks of her as "his" Church. Christ cannot be separated from the Church any more than the head can be separated from the body (cf. *1 Cor* 12:12). The Church does not draw her life from herself, but from the Lord.

We cannot follow Jesus on our own

Dear young friends, as the Successor of Peter, let me urge you to strengthen this faith which has been handed down to us from the time of the Apostles. Make Christ, the Son of God, the centre of your life. But let me also remind you that following Jesus in faith means walking at his side in the communion of the Church. We cannot follow Jesus on our own. Anyone who would be tempted to do so "on his own", or to approach the life of faith with that kind of individualism so prevalent today, will risk never truly encountering Jesus, or will end up following a counterfeit Jesus.

Having faith means drawing support from the faith of your brothers and sisters, even as your own faith serves as a support for the faith of others. I ask you, dear friends, to love the Church which brought you to birth in the faith, which helped you to grow in the knowledge of Christ and which led you to discover the beauty of his love. Growing in friendship with Christ necessarily means recognizing the importance of joyful participation in the life of your parishes, communities and movements, as well as the celebration of Sunday Mass, frequent reception of the sacrament of Reconciliation, and the cultivation of personal prayer and meditation on God's word.

Share the joy of your faith

Friendship with Jesus will also lead you to bear witness to the faith wherever you are, even when it meets with rejection or indifference. We cannot encounter Christ and not want to make him known to others. So do not keep Christ to yourselves! Share with others the joy of your faith. The world needs the witness of your faith, it surely needs God. I think that the presence here of so many young people, coming from all over the world, is a wonderful proof of the fruitfulness of Christ's command to the Church: "Go into all the world and proclaim the Gospel to the whole creation" (*Mk* 16:15). You too have been given the extraordinary task of being disciples and missionaries of Christ in other lands and countries filled with young people who are looking for something greater and, because their heart tells them that more authentic values do exist, they do not let themselves be seduced by the empty promises of a lifestyle which has no room for God.

I pray for you with heartfelt affection. I commend all of you to the Virgin Mary and I ask her to accompany you always by her maternal intercession and to teach you how to remain faithful to God's word. I ask you to pray for the Pope, so that, as the Successor of Peter, he may always

confirm his brothers and sisters in the faith. May all of us in the Church, pastors and faithful alike, draw closer to the Lord each day. May we grow in holiness of life and be effective witnesses to the truth that Jesus Christ is indeed the Son of God, the Saviour of all mankind and the living source of our hope. Amen.

The feast of faith

The time has come for us to say good-bye. These days spent in Madrid, in the company of so many young people from Spain and from throughout the world, will remain deeply etched in my mind and heart.

Your Majesty, the Pope felt at home in Spain! And the young people who were the heart of this World Youth Day found a warm welcome here and in the many cities and towns of the country, which they were able to visit in the days before these celebrations. ...

Spain is a great nation whose soundly open, pluralistic and respectful society is capable of moving forward without surrendering its profoundly religious and Catholic soul. In these days, it once more made this clear, revealing its technical and human resources in the service of an undertaking of immense consequence and promise: that of helping young people to become more deeply rooted in Jesus Christ, our Saviour. ...

I leave Spain very happy and grateful to everyone. But above all I am grateful to God, our Lord, who allowed me to celebrate these days so filled with enthusiasm and grace, so charged with dynamism and hope. The feast of faith which we have shared enables us to look forward with great confidence in Providence, which guides the Church across the seas of history. That is why she continues to be young and full of life, even as she confronts challenging situations. This is the work of the Holy Spirit, who makes Jesus Christ present in the hearts of young people in every age and shows them the grandeur of the divine vocation given to every man and woman. We were also able to see how the grace of Christ tears down the walls and overcomes the barriers which sin erects between peoples and generations, in order to make all mankind a single family which acknowledges its one Father and which cultivates, by work and respect, all that he has given us in creation.

Missionaries of the Gospel

Young people readily respond when one proposes to them, in sincerity and truth, an encounter with Jesus Christ, the one Redeemer of humanity. Now those young people are returning home as missionaries of the Gospel, "rooted and built up in Christ, and firm in the faith", and they will need to be helped on their way. So I urge Bishops, priests, Religious and Christian educators in particular, to care for those young people who want to respond enthusiastically to the Lord's call. There is no reason to lose heart in the face of the various obstacles we encounter in some countries. The yearning for God which the Creator has placed in the hearts of young people is more powerful than all of these, as is the power from on high which gives divine strength to those who follow the Master and who seek in him nourishment for life. Do not be afraid to present to young people the message of Jesus Christ in all its integrity, and to invite them to celebrate the sacraments by which he gives us a share in his own life.

Your Majesty, before returning to Rome, I would like to assure the people of Spain of my constant prayers, especially for married couples and families who are facing various kinds of difficulties, the needy and the infirm, the elderly and children, as well as those who have no work. I pray in particular of the young people of Spain. I am sure that they will contribute the best they have to offer through their faith in Christ, so that this great country can face the challenges of the present hour and can continue along the paths of peace, solidarity, justice and freedom. Along with these intentions, I entrust the sons and daughters of this noble land to the intercession of the Virgin Mary, our heavenly Mother, and to them all I willingly impart my blessing. May the joy of the Lord always fill your hearts. Thank you.

Sources

This booklet draws together homilies and addresses of Pope Benedict XVI, made during World Youth Day 2011 in Madrid.

Our deepest identity is in Christ: Message of His Holiness Pope Benedict XVI, For The Twenty-Sixth World Youth Day (2011), From The Vatican, 6 August 2010, Feast Of The Transfiguration Of The Lord.

The strength of faith: Welcome Ceremony, Address of His Holiness Benedict XVI, International Airport of Madrid, Barajas, Thursday, 18 August 2011.

Our foundations are in Christ: Welcome Ceremony with Young People, Address of His Holiness Benedict XVI, Plaza De Cibeles, Madrid, Thursday, 18 August 2011.

Consecrated to Christ with an undivided heart: Meeting with Young Women Religious, Address of His Holiness Benedict XVI, Monastery of San Lorenzo De El Escorial, Friday, 19 August 2011.

Spreading the truth of Christ: Meeting with Young University Professors, Address Of His Holiness Benedict XVI, Basilica of The Monastery of San Lorenzo De El Escorial, Friday, 19 August 2011.

Mysterious wisdom of the Cross: The Way of The Cross, Address Of His Holiness Benedict XVI, Plaza De Cibeles, Madrid, Friday, 19 August 2011.

Prepare to become Apostles: Eucharist With Seminarians, Homily Of His Holiness Benedict XVI, Cathedral Of Santa María La Real De La Almudena, Madrid, Saturday, 20 August 2011.

How to embrace suffering: Visit to the San José Foundation, Greeting of His Holiness Benedict XVI, Madrid, Saturday, 20 August 2011.

Faith elevates and perfects your ideals: Prayer Vigil with Young People , Homily of His Holiness Benedict XVI , Cuatro Vientos Air Base, Madrid , Saturday, 20 August 2011.

Ways of knowing Christ: Final Mass, Words of The Holy Father at The Beginning of The Eucharistic Celebration, And Homily, Cuatro Vientos Air Base, Madrid , Sunday, 21 August 2011.

The feast of faith: Departure Ceremony, Address of His Holiness Benedict XVI , International Airport of Madrid Barajas, Sunday, 21 August 201.

Acknowledgement

The pictures in this booklet are from the winners of a competition run by the CTS on its Facebook page following World Youth Day. We would like to thank all of those who participated for their submissions, we hope they help to give a flavour of what it was like to personally participate in this important historical event for the Church and the world.

CI

Be

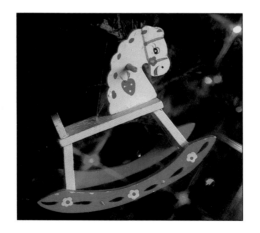

A LION BOOK

Oxford · Batavia · Sydney

Published by
Lion Publishing plc
Sandy Lane West, Littlemore, Oxford, England
ISBN 0 7459 1607 4
Albatross Books Pty Ltd
PO Box 320, Sutherland, NSW 2232, Australia
ISBN 07324 0065 1

First edition 1989

Acknowledgments
Photographs by Susanna Burton, pages 29, 40; The Image
Bank /Brett Froomer, pages 1, 8 /Alvis Upitis, page 12 /Marti Pie,
page 17 /Bill Carter, page 33 /Colin Molyneux, page 44–45;
Lion Publishing/Jon Willcocks, page 25; Zefa (UK) Ltd, page 20.

Printed and bound in Yugoslavia

CONTENTS

1

The End of a Dream

For most people, having a baby is as natural as breathing air. Becoming pregnant calls for nothing more than normal marital relations.

For husbands and wives who are infertile, however, nothing seems to work properly. Their bodies do not cooperate by producing a fertilized egg. Or, when an egg is fertilized, the unborn baby is lost through miscarriage.

If you are childless, you may feel betrayed by your body, cheated out of an experience that comes easily to others. Your life and marriage seem at a dead end.

Without the children you long to have, you may face uncertainty and frustration about every major decision in your life. What sort of future will you plan for now? Where will you live and where will you work?

Meanwhile, your emotions begin to fray. Husband and wife may blame one another and feel hurt, angry and sad. No one who knows you may understand the depth or the source of your pain.

When your dream begins to die, you feel alone and in despair. Infertility hurts, maybe even more than other marital difficulties, because every 28 days, when conception fails, the wounds open again.

As your infertility drags on for months or years, you may begin to think that your life and marriage will never be 'normal'.

Eventually many childless couples become parents through medical treatment or adoption. Others decide against further treatment, accepting the fact that they may never have a child.

In the meantime, however, the emotional and marital strain of infertility needs to be resolved.

How can you cope with all the myths and misunderstanding that surround childlessness today? Are you meant to have children? How will you know if you ought to adopt? Why do some people become parents only to abort or abuse or neglect their children? Are you being punished?

Fortunately, there is hope. There is a path to resolving the infertility crisis, though it is neither short nor easy. It begins when you honestly acknowledge your feelings and the medical realities.

Understanding infertility does not take away the pain, but it can direct your steps towards the road to recovery.

2

The Myths

'Just relax.'

'Adopt a child, and then you'll have one of your own.'

'Stop trying so hard.'

'Take a long holiday . . . then you'll get pregnant.'

'God must be punishing you.'

If you are childless, you have probably heard a steady chorus of comments like these from well-meaning friends and relatives. For most childless couples infertility is a medical problem. Yet for some reason it invites suggested remedies that would never be offered to someone with arthritis, a malfunctioning kidney, or a heart murmur!

Often, people who do not know very much about infertility believe it is an emotional or a psychological problem. Even in medical circles, this view was common until the 1940s. Improvements in medical knowledge and technique have made this view obsolete. Infertility is now recognized as a physical problem that can be traced to the man, the woman, or both partners in most cases.

When someone tells you to relax, take a holiday or stop worrying, they seem to imply that you need to be in the right frame of mind to become pregnant. If this were true, why are there so many unwanted pregnancies? How could rape result in pregnancy if a woman needs to be relaxed to conceive? How easy birth control would be if a woman only had to get nervous to keep from getting pregnant!

When someone tells you to relax, do not hesitate to point out that relaxation is no cure for infertility. Infertility causes stress, but normal day-to-day tension does not cause infertility.

Another common myth involves adoption. Almost everyone knows someone who adopted a child and then became pregnant, often with twins or even triplets! Certainly this happens. Unexpected pregnancies also occur — in about the same proportion — among formerly infertile couples who do not adopt. The vast majority of adoptive parents do not find their physical infertility miraculously resolved.

The idea that adoption will help you become pregnant demeans the adopted child. It makes it sound as if you would adopt a child in order to insure a future pregnancy, and not because you simply love the adopted child for his or her own sake. Adoption is a possibility to consider after you have come to terms with the pain and grief of infertility. It is not a short cut to fertility.

Infertile couples often feel like failures — worthless as people — because they are unable to have children. That feeling can be magnified unbearably if someone suggests that God may be punishing you. Like the other myths, this idea is absolutely wrong. God is not like that. He loves and cares for

every one of us. He does not punish us for some unknown sin.

The physical ability to bear a child is no reflection of a couple's human worth or their relationship with God. If it were, children would never be born into circumstances of abuse and neglect. They would not be aborted or abandoned.

3

What Is Really the Matter?

□ Carol and Dan both visited doctors to find out why they could not conceive. They were stunned at the report they received from Dan's doctor. Dan had a rare condition, present from birth, that kept him from producing any sperm. Dan is *sterile* — absolutely unable to have any part in conception.

□ Linda developed appendicitis, but her doctor mistakenly believed she had the flu. Her appendix ruptured, causing a severe internal infection. As a result, her reproductive organs were damaged. Linda is *infertile* — unlikely to conceive without medical help.

□ Alison and Richard had a lovely daughter soon after their marriage. They planned to have a second child right away, but their son Paul was not born until nine agonizing years had passed. They suffered from *secondary infertility*.

My husband and I tried to conceive for four frustrating years before we sought thorough medical help. Time and time again, we were dismayed when the doctors found nothing seriously wrong with either of us. A pregnancy has never happened, and we do not know why.

There are many different types of infertility. As

a general rule, if you do not conceive after one year of normal sexual relations you may be considered infertile. Women who repeatedly conceive and then miscarry are also considered infertile.

Sometimes solving infertility means making a simple change in behaviour. A couple may not have sexual relations often enough to make it likely that they will conceive. Or they may need to time their relations more exactly to match the woman's most fertile days of the month.

Age can be a factor in infertility. Women generally reach the peak of fertility in their mid-twenties. After thirty, their chances of becoming pregnant decrease.

Poor nutrition, alcohol or drug abuse, and sexually transmitted diseases contribute to infertility as well.

About one-third of all infertile couples trace their physical problem directly to the man, another third to the woman. Often it is a treatable problem.

For most of the remaining third, infertility results from a combination of problems. Again, many of these can be treated. In fact, about half of the couples who seek medical help for infertility eventually achieve pregnancy. Only a small percentage of infertile couples cannot be diagnosed.

'What's really the matter?' you may be asking as you begin to cope with infertility. Be encouraged: a doctor probably has the answer. Set aside your embarrassment, frustration and shame. Make an appointment and find out.

4

A Couple's Concern

If you are a woman, infertility may deal you a harsher emotional blow than your husband experiences. You are the one who may miss out on being pregnant and giving birth. Usually it is the woman's daily life that changes most if a child is born.

Because of the strength of traditional roles, a woman's sense of identity and value may be more deeply damaged if she is unable to become a mother.

Nonetheless, infertility is a couple's concern. Husbands have deep needs and feelings too. It is important for everyone's sake that husbands stay actively involved, and that you work through your infertility together.

Infertile couples often feel isolated from the fertile world. Women who cannot conceive may find Mother's Day, a christening in church, or visiting a new mother and baby excruciatingly painful. Your female friends and relatives may talk about their own pregnancies and children, or ask why you are not 'getting started'. Retreating to the comfort and understanding of your partner is extremely important at times like these.

Barbara and Paul, who experienced more than ten years of infertility before they adopted a child, found ways to support one another. 'Paul went through all the monthly ups and downs with me,' Barbara recalls, 'serving as a good friend and counsellor.'

Infertility can threaten the happiest husbands and wives. A man in his late thirties wistfully says, 'Although we love one another very much, not having children has been the missing link in our marriage — a problem that has been very difficult to deal with. At times we wonder whether our relationship can endure the strain.'

Married partners who are able to discuss infertility openly, share their deepest feelings, and understand how it is affecting both of them, find the experience can draw them closer. A husband's cooperation and sympathetic understanding mean more to a wife than any other gesture of caring.

And when a wife recognizes her husband's need to stay focused on his work and other interests, she begins to put the important goal of parenting into perspective with other aspirations.

As you seek medical treatment, it is essential that both husband and wife participate in the process. The man as well as the woman must be willing to visit a doctor and perhaps undergo treatment.

A man needs to be especially tolerant of the ways in which infertility treatments may affect the couple's sexual relationship. The need to schedule relations for a wife's most fertile days may continue for months and even years. Without a husband's patient support and enthusiasm, sex can become a source of severe misunderstanding and tension for an infertile couple.

Men are often able to bring a sorely needed touch of humour to the situation. One man jokingly called his time of infertility 'wait training'. Another got his wife laughing by suggesting that she turn the tables on her fertile friends. 'Tell them they are just too relaxed — that's why they have so many children!'

A full medical evaluation for an infertile couple cannot take place successfully if either the husband or wife is uncooperative. And to let one partner carry the emotional burden of infertility is simply unfair. Sharing the turmoil of childlessness together will deepen your commitment to each other, whether you eventually give birth to a child, adopt a child, or decide to accept the no-children option.

5

Surprise and Denial

'This can't be happening to us!'

'Surely I'll be pregnant by this time next month.'

No two couples experience infertility in exactly the same way. Still, counsellors and doctors have identified a number of emotional phases through which practically every infertile couple will pass. Once you know this, often you can pinpoint how far you have already travelled along the road to resolution.

Infertility triggers a grief cycle in the lives of couples who desire children. Yet it is often a grief denied, either by themselves or by friends or relatives who do not understand the reality of their loss.

No one has actually died, after all. There is no ceremony, no funeral for the longed-for child who does not come. Still, the infertile couple must grieve.

Usually grieving begins with the startling first awareness that you have a new — and unwelcome — addition to your identity. You are infertile. You greet this new knowledge just as you would the news of a chronic illness or handicap. You are profoundly surprised. And you are likely to deny it.

For a while, denial serves as a healthy defence. It allows a couple to come to grips with their infertility

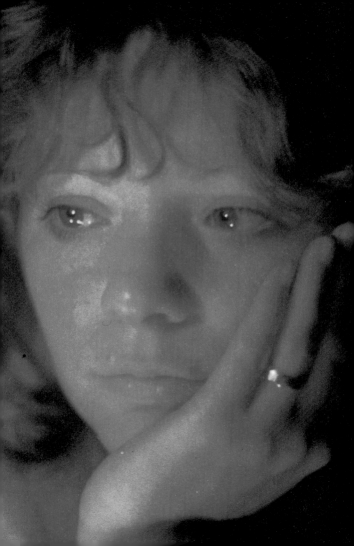

a little at a time. The overwhelming sense of loss may be too much to cope with all at once. Keeping hope alive, if only for another month or two, lets you adjust to this new reality in your own time.

In some cases, no physical cause for infertility is identified. In these cases, the grief is different. A spark of hope for pregnancy may never go away completely. The couple's longing for a child may resemble the feelings of a family awaiting news of a soldier missing in action.

Feeling surprised about infertility is only the first of a series of emotions that accompany childlessness. Denying the unpleasant truth is an early way of coping with it. The next emotions most infertile couples experience are much more threatening to emotional well-being.

6

Anger and Depression

Once the reality of infertility is no longer a surprise and is too real to be denied, you may find that you are profoundly angry.

What makes you angry is not a specific person or event, but rather a life process that is interrupted and a goal that is blocked. There is nothing and no one to blame for infertility, so anger finds other targets.

Husband and wife may lash out at one another, accusing each other of being insensitive or missing opportunities to conceive. A doctor or a nurse may be the undeserving target. Often couples are surprised by their intense feelings of anger towards family members or friends who have children.

Holidays and other occasions which are focused on children may provoke uncomfortable outbursts. Christmastime was especially difficult for Barbara. It was difficult enough, year after year, to celebrate the birth of the baby Jesus. Seeing her younger brother, his wife and their newborn son at a family gathering stirred an uncharacteristic rage in her. She yelled at her mother, 'I'm never coming home again!'

Anger is a natural reaction when you feel that the circumstances of your life are out of control. Infertility brings with it a deep sense of helplessness.

Life no longer seems predictable or manageable. You may be overwhelmed by the unfairness of it all.

Eventually, anger gives way to depression. You may enter a time of deep sorrow, despair and exhaustion. Everything in life seems pointless. You lack the energy to perform well at your job or other duties.

'I cried inside almost constantly, and the slightest nudge to my emotions would bring the tears out,' one young woman admitted. 'One day, while driving, I noticed a woman in the car ahead of me talking to a baby in a car seat. Stopped at a red light, she was pointing out sights by the road as the baby's tiny fists bounced excitedly up and down. I cried so hard I could hardly continue driving.'

Depression is a serious condition. If it is indeed the result of your infertility, it will be temporary. The black clouds will lift eventually and you will be one step closer to resolution.

If depression is a result of unexpressed anger or guilt about infertility, or if it arises from more deep-seated sources than infertility, you may require professional help.

Anger and depression are powerful feelings. They should not be ignored or denied or bottled up. The best way to cope with them is to pause for a moment and recognize what is going on inside you. Then tell a trusted friend, a counsellor or your partner. In the retelling, even the most potent bad feelings lose their punch. Expressing anger and sorrow verbally is a healthy way to let them go.

It may not happen just once. Waves of feeling

may continue to overwhelm you, triggered by new circumstances, a thoughtless comment, or more months with no pregnancy.

If this happens, it is nothing to worry about. Keep on talking about those feelings until they begin to fade again. When only a trace of them colours your outlook on yourself and the world around you, you are ready for the grief that heals.

7

Grief That Heals

Grief comes to a couple when they first realize that pregnancy will probably not occur naturally for them. It includes surprise, denial, anger and depression as well as open sorrow and mourning. It is an extremely unpleasant state to be in, but it is necessary, because it promotes healed emotions.

Grief does not destroy the memory of the loss, but it leaves you knowing more about yourself. New depths of feeling are plumbed, and new awareness of the pain of others develops. Grief is a friend, not an enemy.

A grieving couple sorrows for the loss of their longed-for child, for the choices about family life that they cannot make, for the loss of pregnancy and childbirth and breast-feeding. The grief is often accompanied by physical symptoms including uncontrolled weeping and loss of appetite.

The work of grieving involves reviewing feelings about the loss you have suffered. Over and over again, the circumstances of your infertility and your desire for a child play through your minds. Often this lasts for several months, or more. Sorrow may return unexpectedly for years, like an old friend paying a visit.

It may be even more difficult for a couple who

can conceive but then lose the child before birth. A woman who miscarries mourns her loss as much as a woman who loses an infant after birth.

Finally, the tightly tangled feelings of grief ease and separate into more orderly patterns of thought and emotion. When this begins to happen, you are approaching recovery. You begin to feel enthusiasm again for your daily activities.

Energy returns and relationships are re-established. You welcome back a sense of satisfaction, joy, laughter and warmth.

You may still long for a child, but that desire does not overshadow every other pursuit. You begin to live with your infertility as an accepted part of yourself. Questions about why you are infertile do not occur to you as often as they used to.

But what about the difficult questions infertility raises? Grieving may heal the emotional wounds, but it doesn't offer any solid answers. To whom can you turn?

8

Finding Support

The expression of grief involves talking out your feelings until they no longer dominate every waking thought. It is good to talk to your partner about your struggles with isolation, surprise, anger and depression. As you share the pain of infertility, you will grow in intimacy.

Problems can arise, though, if you are talking

only with your partner. There comes a time when everything that can be said has been said. Even the most tolerant wife or husband can't help tuning out the repetition.

Paul and Barbara, who helped each other through ten years of waiting for a child, found it was not always easy. Paul confesses, 'There were times when I felt I could not tolerate another tirade on the baby situation. We had to discuss other topics to maintain balance.'

You need at least one other sympathetic pair of listening ears. Often a clergyman or family counsellor can help. However, they usually have no special training concerning infertility. When my husband and I visited a counsellor for help in sorting out our feelings and questions about infertility, we were amazed to hear him joke about our situation. 'You can borrow my children any time,' he laughingly told us.

Our best source of ongoing support was a small group of couples also experiencing infertility. Each of them had arrived at a different point on the road to resolution. Several had already adopted or given birth, and they met with us to offer hope and encouragement.

Even if you meet with only one other couple going through the same struggle, it can be a tremendous source of comfort and stability. It reinforces the fact that you are not alone. About one couple in six struggles at some point in their marriage with infertility.

Alison, who endured nine years of waiting and testing before she could have a second child, met on Friday mornings with a group of women who studied the Bible together and prayed. In those meetings, Alison's friends gently helped her let go of her anxieties and preoccupation with pregnancy. The emotional wounds of infertility healed well before she had her long-awaited second baby.

Carol and Dan continued to want a child, but they were terribly uncertain about adoption. They began attending a support group started by their church. As they spoke openly and honestly about their fears, other couples who had already adopted offered suggestions and reassurance. Sooner than they ever imagined, Carol and Dan brought home a lovely five-week-old boy, adopted through an agency near them.

In the midst of all the frustration, it is difficult to find answers to the deepest questions. The fog of pain and confusion is too dense to permit any light to shine on the areas that trouble you most.

That is why you need to have the support of a few caring friends. Don't expect them to have easy answers for you. But answers will begin to emerge as you share your feelings and thoughts with them.

9

Are We Being Punished?

Many people wonder if some past behaviour or attitude is preventing conception.

Perhaps you used birth control before you discovered you were infertile, and you wonder if you hurt yourself or waited too long. Or maybe there is an abortion or an affair in your past that still troubles you emotionally.

For many infertile couples, the question comes in the context of their religious belief. Is God angry with us? Is he punishing us by not letting us have children?

Infertility generates feelings of guilt and worthlessness. You may find yourself bargaining with God, promising anything in exchange for a child.

This goes back at least as far as Bible times. Hannah, longing for a child, prays: 'O Lord Almighty, if you will only look upon your servant's misery and remember me, and not forget your servant but give her a son, then I will give him to the Lord for all the days of his life.'

Hannah was an outstanding and faithful wife. Nothing in the Bible story suggests she was being punished with infertility.

In the New Testament, Zechariah and Elizabeth,

the parents of John the Baptist, were also childless for many years. The Gospel of Luke says, 'Both of them were upright in the sight of God, observing all the Lord's commandments and regulations blamelessly. But they had no children, because Elizabeth was barren; and they were both well on in years.'

There is no connection between a person's worth and his or her fertility.

God is intimately involved with the creation of new life. Trying to discern all the reasons why certain people have children and certain people do not is an exercise in futility, however. No one can fully comprehend why God acts in particular ways or what he intends to accomplish.

We can be sure, though, that infertility does *not* mean we are being punished.

On the contrary, the Bible assures us of God's love for us. He does not always change the difficult circumstances of our lives, but he offers us strength and courage to meet them.

God has a special purpose for each one of us. He will open up all sorts of possibilities if we place our lives in his hands and ask him to guide us.

To some childless couples he will give children, whether through birth or adoption. To others he will give other goals, other duties, other joys. And to all who commit their lives to him, he will give peace and joy.

10

Are We Meant to Be Parents?

Once a sense of guilt and worthlessness subsides, you may still find yourself asking, *Why?* Why can't we have any children?

No other question stirs more anguish and uncertainty. Asking why, though, is an important step in the necessary — but painful — work of grief. 'Are we meant to be parents?' is a question you may raise with your partner, your friends and family, or a counsellor or clergyman.

This is a starting point for serious discussion about your future. You are infertile. So now what will you do?

You are beginning, ever so slowly, to look ahead. Instead of dwelling sorrowfully on your past and present inability ever to become pregnant or carry a child, you are setting your sights on future options.

If your future together does not include children, that is not the end of your life or marriage. You still have all the talents, skills and interests you had before you discovered your infertility.

Best of all, you have each other. Are you meant to be parents? Most married couples assume that they are.

If the desire for a child remains insistent, if you keep longing for a baby, if you feel positively unfulfilled without one, then you are perfectly normal. The chances are that you would be a wonderful parent, because devotion to a child is what matters most in parenting. Even though you struggle with self-doubts because of your infertility, you are probably well-equipped to bring up a child.

On the other hand, your desire for a child may fade as you undergo medical testing. When the grief has passed, you and your partner may find — to your surprise — that you really value other activities and goals more than parenting. This is normal as well. No married couple is required to have children. Or you may decide that, much as you long for children, this should no longer be your main preoccupation. Positively, you may ask, is there some other task that we are meant to do as a married couple?

The important thing is to sort out your feelings honestly. Listen to your own heart and to one another. Benefit from the wisdom and counsel of others. You will know whether you are meant to be parents.

Those who have that certainty will be able to look into an alternative such as adoption, and to stick with it through an often lengthy and difficult process.

11

What Makes a Family?

'When are you two going to start your family?'

This innocent question usually comes very early on — and it can hurt. It suggests that the two of you are not a family already. So it is important to stop at this point and ask what makes a family.

The first thing to say is that your family got started on your wedding day!

Western society's understanding of marriage and family is drawn primarily from the Bible. But even though the Bible values childbearing, it never suggests that children are essential to a marriage.

A marriage is created, according to the book of Genesis, when a man leaves his father and mother and is united with his wife. Children are never identified as a necessary fulfilment for marriage. They are seen instead as a blessing and a gift — but one that not every couple receives.

Besides, a married couple, with or without children, is not an isolated unit. Husband and wife are set in the midst of parents and grandparents, aunts and uncles, sisters and brothers and cousins and nieces and nephews. This too is family.

The Bible speaks of yet another family — God's family. It compares God to a caring father, a loving husband. It calls Jesus our brother. It says that if we put our faith in Jesus, other believers are our brothers and sisters! We belong to a family that includes all races and colours, that reaches around the world.

Real families are not made simply by giving birth. Cats and dogs give birth, but they do not form families. Families are made through love and commitment, through unselfish caring for others' needs.

So what do you say to the insensitive questioner? You may wish to use a polite equivalent of 'none of your business.' Or you may just smile and say, 'Whatever can you mean? We've been a family for years.'

12

Alternatives for Childless Couples

Encouragement from others is important while you sort out your feelings about infertility. It continues to help as you weigh various alternatives to childlessness.

Often, a doctor will tell an infertile couple about a variety of high-technology alternatives.

☐ One option, *artificial insemination*, has been used for many years. This medical procedure, done in a doctor's office, involves taking a semen sample from the husband or from an anonymous donor and injecting it into the wife's vagina when fertilization is most likely.

The use of sperm from a donor raises difficult ethical questions. It violates the exclusive union of husband and wife. It also requires a decision about telling the child his or her true parentage. The Catholic church opposes all artificial means of conception, including artificial insemination with the husband's sperm.

☐ A newer procedure, *in vitro fertilization*, has gained popularity rapidly ever since 'test-tube baby' Louise Brown was born in 1978. This process involves taking sperm from the husband and eggs from the wife, and mixing them together in a laboratory. Any fertilized eggs that result are placed back inside the woman.

In vitro fertilization is very expensive, and the success rate is rarely better than 20 per cent. It raises a host of ethical questions as well, especially if some fertilized eggs are discarded or frozen for future use. What are the rights of these tiny embryos, which have the full capacity to become human beings?

☐ Occasionally, a couple will hire a *surrogate mother* to bear a child for them. In this way, the child is biologically related to the husband, whose sperm is used to artificially inseminate the surrogate. The people who arrange such match-ups generally charge the infertile couple an enormous sum of money and the woman who bears the baby receives a large fee for her services.

This alternative is far different from adoption, because the child's conception and separation from the mother are prearranged. The woman who bears the child is often poor, seeing surrogacy as a desperate way to earn money. She then finds herself legally bound to give up her child, with no chance to change her mind. Surrogate arrangements are only a step removed from baby-selling.

Finally, there are two options that offer hope for infertile couples in very different ways. One is adoption. The other is to accept the lack of children, determining to make the most of a 'child-free' life.

13

Adoption

Adoption is an alternative considered by many childless couples as they seek to add children to their families. It means taking into your home a biologically unrelated child, and raising and loving that child as your own.

In a legal adoption, the woman who gives birth to the child freely decides to place him or her with another family, usually because she feels it would be impossible to raise the child herself at that particular time in her life.

Some adoptions are accomplished independently, when an infertile couple directly contact a pregnant woman who wants to place her child with them. Often they are assisted by a lawyer, doctor, or clergyman.

Other adoptions are handled by public or private agencies. In most cases, fees are charged to cover administrative costs, counselling for the birth-mother, and sometimes her medical expenses.

Some couples do not investigate adoption because they have heard that few infants are available to be adopted. This is true: adoption is more difficult today than it was a generation or two ago. Many children conceived out of wedlock are aborted, and most of those that are born are kept by their mothers

In addition, infertility seems to be increasing.

Still, persistent couples continue to adopt infants. Some decide to adopt a child of another race or from another country. Some adopt older children. And some still find babies through adoption agencies. If adoption interests you, talk to people who have recently adopted. Most are happy to share any helpful information they have discovered.

Adoption offers a wonderful alternative for millions of childless couples. It is a happy solution to their years of frustration over infertility. They find, though, that adoption brings with it some new emotional issues that need to be faced.

Preparing to adopt means accepting the fact that your child may not look or act like anyone on either side of the family tree. There may be resistance from some family members. As your child matures and begins to ask questions, you must be ready with answers that are truthful and compassionate. And one day, the child may want to search for a long-lost birth-mother.

Do these aspects of the adoption decision trouble you? It is normal to have concerns and questions about such a major life decision. An adoption agency representative can help you think them through.

Many childless couples wonder whether they will be able to love an adopted child who comes into their home as a total stranger. Don't forget that biological parents have to get acquainted with their newborns as well!

Building a bond of love with a child is not something that happens magically through birth or

breastfeeding. Instead it is a process of developing mutual trust and affection.

How will you know when to go ahead and apply to adopt?

☐ When you view pregnancy as one small fraction of parenting, and you realize parenting is your true goal.

☐ When the thought that your biological 'dream child' will never exist no longer causes fresh pain, and you can put that thought in your past.

☐ When an end to medical treatment seems more like a relief than like giving up.

☐ When adoption emerges as a positive choice you can make for yourselves, rather than a last resort.

☐ When you both know in your hearts that you can love a genetically unrelated child as your own, for ever.

14

Remaining Child Free

If serious uncertainties about medical options and adoption linger even after you have put to rest the emotions of infertility, you have another alternative. Perhaps it would be best for you to remain child free.

This term is used deliberately instead of the well-worn term *childless*. Being child free indicates a positive decision on your part. It is not just an inevitable surrender to circumstances. Nor is it a selfish choice made from unwillingness to accept the responsibility of parenting. It needs emotional healing from the shock of infertility. It demands an ability to look confidently and enthusiastically ahead towards a future without children of your own.

This certainly should not mean that out of hurt you cut yourselves off from children or teenagers. Just the opposite. You can make the most of opportunities to make friends with your nephews and nieces. You can help out with the children at church, or befriend a neighbour's children who need more adult companionship than their parents can provide. As you do so, pain quickly gives way to joy, delight and enrichment.

A retired couple, Bill and Sylvia, look back on a fulfilling life without children. Together they have sponsored a number of needy children in another country. They have built strong, lasting relationships with nieces and nephews. They have invested time and energy in significant volunteer programmes.

Once the grief of infertility was behind them, they took every available opportunity to embrace life. They looked ahead, not back.

Embracing life, for the majority of child-free couples, means examining their abilities, interests and resources and committing themselves to a life of worthwhile work and service, whether through their jobs or through other activities. It means looking beyond themselves to others' needs, realizing that lasting joy comes from what we give, not what we get.

Making a choice for child-free living is not easy, and it may take a long time. When the choice is made, insensitive comments from others can still hurt. People who do not understand may suggest you are too selfish or too ambitious to have children.

Just keep in mind that you do not owe an explanation to anyone. If infertility is best resolved for you by a choice to remain child free, then by all means make that decision.

15

New Depths of Compassion

'I'm so tired of this. I wish I didn't even want children!'

When you hit the bottom emotionally because of childlessness, you may wonder why you were ever

plagued with the desire for children in the first place. 'Why doesn't God take away this longing for a child if it's never going to happen?'

When despair sets in, it is time for you to try seeing infertility in a larger context. Of course you do not deserve the emotional pain and stress of infertility. You are right when you rail 'It's not fair!' at seeing children born into indifferent or abusive situations.

Suffering hurts, and it is unpleasant. At the same time, it serves a purpose.

If you did not have the capacity to *hurt* deeply

and grieve, you would lack the capacity to rejoice and celebrate. Human beings are not unfeeling robots — thank God! Because of this, we are able to understand and to *help* others in greater need than ourselves.

One young wife, Melinda, captured the essence of this thought in her comment about infertility. 'I'm afraid to let my desire for a child die, because I am afraid of what else might die with it.'

We would cease being ourselves if we shed any of the emotions we are meant to experience.

For infertile couples who believe in a personal, loving God, Job's words in the Bible bring deep comfort. After having lost everything, Job tells God, 'I know that you can do all things; no plan of yours can be thwarted.'

Job focused his thoughts and his words on God, not on his own circumstances. In the Psalms, King David did the same thing when he wrote, 'Whom have I in heaven but you? And being with you, I desire nothing on earth. My flesh and my heart may fail, but God is the strength of my heart and my portion for ever.'

Your flesh may fail you by refusing to produce a child. You may feel that your heart — your very being — will fail as well from sorrow. But there is more to life than flesh and feelings. There is a very real God who is intensely interested in the choices human beings make.

He will love you regardless of whether you bear children, adopt children, or remain child free.

He does not arbitrarily grant children to some

couples and withhold them from others. His plans and his ways are beyond our ability to understand even dimly. But we know beyond a doubt that he is there to hurt with us, guide us, and comfort us through life's roughest passages.

As infertility becomes part of your past and not your present, you may glimpse within yourself new depths of compassion and sensitivity. You may find a new capacity to love a needy child, permanently through adoption or temporarily through foster care or social programmes.

Take comfort in the knowledge that infertility can give something back to you, even if it robs you of what you believe you need and desire most in all the world. In the world as we know it, suffering is part of the fabric of life. But God suffers with his children, and he will show them the way to healing.

This may seem very difficult, but can you thank God for what he is accomplishing in you through your infertility? Can you begin to identify positive ways this uninvited pain has changed you?

This is the hope of infertility. Hope keeps alive the flicker of a possibility that good can come out of bad, even in the bleakest situation.

Don't let despair trap you and feed on you as you come to grips with childlessness. Reach out to people around you, people who love you and care about you. Let them help you break free from anger, depression and guilt. With their advice and encouragement, make the choice that suits you best.

Then rejoice! You have successfully navigated one of life's darkest paths. You are on your way again.